I am Woman, I am Invincible, I am Tired...

 PETER PAUPER PRESS, INC.
White Plains, New York

Born to Shop®

Book designed by Heather Zschock

Published by Peter Pauper Press, Inc.
202 Mamaroneck Avenue
White Plains, NY 10601
All rights reserved
ISBN 978-1-59359-933-1
Printed in China
21 20 19 18 17

Visit us at www.peterpauper.com

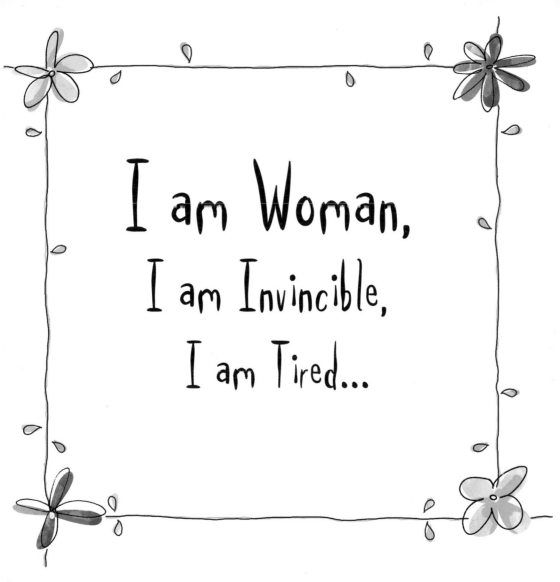

Contents

Introduction

If your coping mechanisms involve chocolate, martinis, and witty friends, you're in good company! Life is too short to drink bad wine, so grab some attitude and delve into these pages filled with the wisdom and wit of like-minded women.

Everyday life may be rife with challenges for the modern woman, but we prevail with our hip humor and sassy sentiments. We may be invincible, but we are also tired; we may be quirky and stressed, but we also know how to live and love large. Here is a book that celebrates you in all your outrageous glory.

Coping with Attitude

I am woman,
I am
invincible,
I am tired...

9

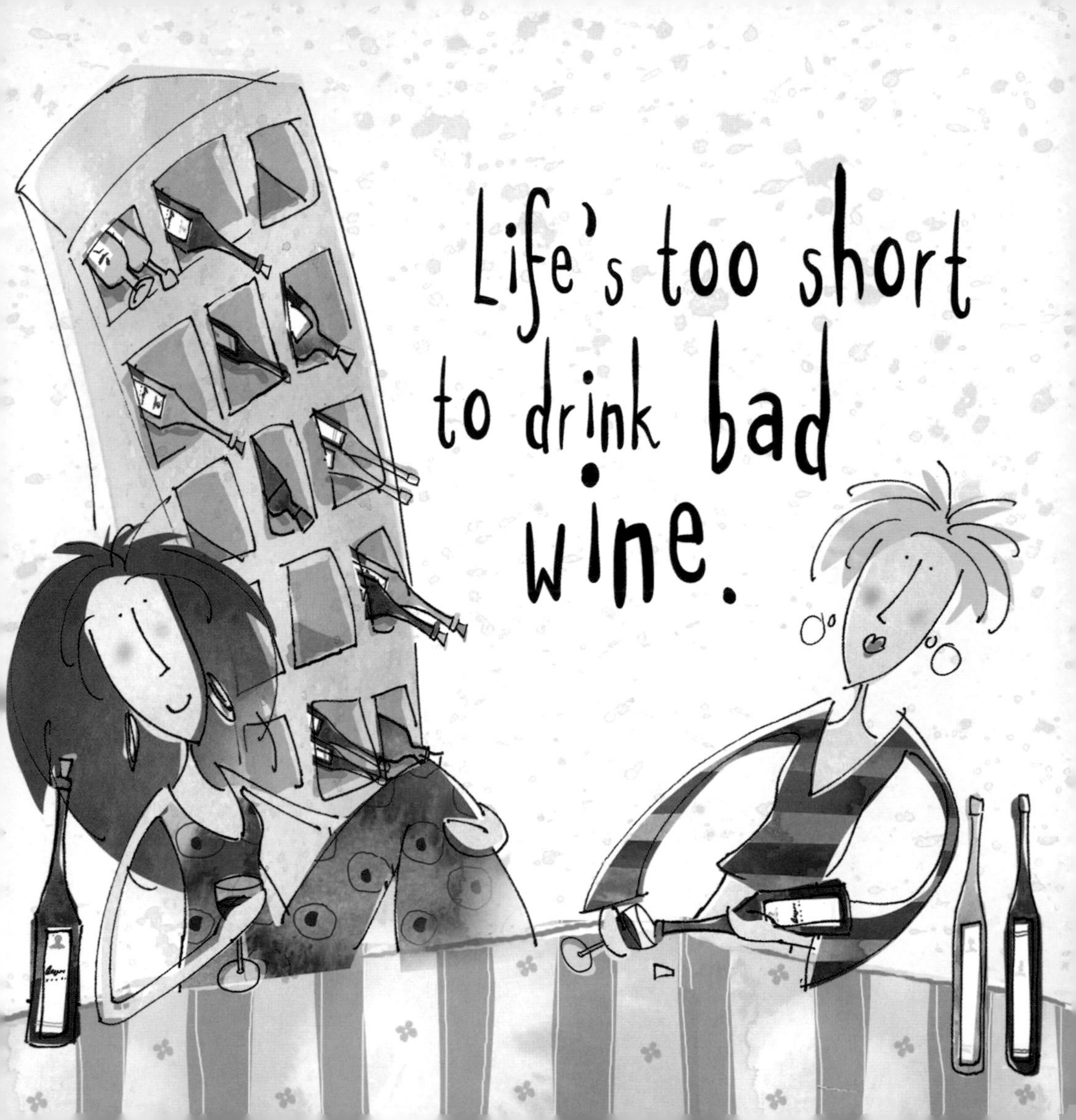
Life's too short
to drink bad
wine.

Seen it all,
done it all,
can't remember
most of it.

Save the Earth—

it's the **only** planet with **chocolate**.

13

When the going gets tough, the tough eat cake.

15

Nine out of ten like chocolate. The tenth person always lies.

At my age a soak in the tub is just a wild night in.

19

21

Whenever I get the urge to exercise, I lie down until the feeling passes.

The **ten** commandments are not **multiple** choice.

Friendship

Friends are the
family
we
choose
for
ourselves.

Friends like you don't grow on trees. I know that this is true, but if friends were flowers there is no doubt how quickly I'd pick you.

Precious and few are friends like you.

You'll always be my friend— you know too much.

31

When friends meet, hearts warm,

Because we can't call people without wings angels, we call them friends.

33

There's nothing better than a good friend, except a good friend with chocolate.

Men and Other Handicaps

37

When I married
Mr. Right,
I didn't
know his
first name
was always.

38

You have to kiss a lot of **frogs** to find a prince.

A little less conversation, a little more action.

41

When I said "I do," I didn't mean everything.

42

I want a man who's kind and understanding. Is that too much to ask of a **millionaire**?

Would you like to
speak to the
man in charge
or the woman who knows
what's happening?

Three things only real men can say: I'm wrong, I'm lost, I can't fix it.

45

Man cannot live by cake alone, but woman can.

Household
Wisdom

49

I love to cook with wine; sometimes I even put it in the food.

flour

53

Many people have eaten in this kitchen and have gone on to live normal healthy lives.

54

A balanced diet is a burger in **each** hand.

55

So it's
not home
sweet
home...
adjust!

56

This life must be a test;
if it were
the real thing
we'd be given
better
instructions.

58

A hug is a great gift— one size fits all.

The best things in life
are the people we love,
the places we've seen,
and the memories
we've made along
the way.

Count your
blessings every day,
before they've grown
and flown away.

It's not what you achieve
in life that
counts, it's how you
get there.

65

Some people make
the world
more special
just by being in it.

I dropped a tear in
the ocean today.
When they find it,
I'll stop loving
you.

Remember that happiness is a means of travel, not a destination.

If you
have
love
you have
everything.

I'm in my own world—
it's ok, they know
me here.

71

Think deeply, speak gently,
love much, laugh aloud,
work hard, give freely,
and be kind.